IF I SHOULD
WAKE
BEFORE I DIE

Your Financial Wake-Up Call:
Everything you should do or would like to do before you die

PAUL A. HARRIS, Clu, Casl

CHARTERED FINANCIAL CONSULTANT

ISBN-10: 1-946203-09-2
ISBN-13: 978-1-946203-09-0

Paul Harris
Paul Harris Financial
4560 Via Royale
Suite 4B

Fort Myers, FL   33919-1076
T: 239.939.5131
F: 239.939.2516
E: info@paulharrisfinancial.com

Expert Press

www.ExpertPress.net

Table of Contents

Dedication

To my beautiful wife, Suzanne, of 34 years,
my son Ryan and his fiancée Uyen
and to my daughter Ashley and her husband Brad.
They all inspire me every day!

Introduction

Allow me to begin by asking you two questions: *What if today was your last day? How important is it to you to have your affairs in order?* This book will be a framework for you to follow in order to put in writing all of your wishes, thoughts, and directions in preparation for your retirement and subsequent death. This book will ensure that the legacy you leave will have a purpose and a clear meaning to those you love.

The questions above are probably questions you don't often hear. However, they are questions that everyone should be asked. It is paramount for every one of us to be financially prepared and ready for any unexpected future event. You may be asking yourself, "What exactly does it mean to be prepared?" According to Webster's Dictionary, to prepare means to "fit, adapt, or qualify for a particular purpose or condition; to make ready". Are you ready?

In the world of business celebrity, the greats whose names spark reactions of admiration, shock, and awe are names such as: Rockefeller, DuPont, Gates, and Jobs. These entrepreneurs are undoubtedly the most widely recognized and spoken of when mentioning financial genius, financial readiness, and overall success.

It would be amiss of me to write a book about financial readiness, however, without first bringing up quite possibly the most important word to understand when it comes to being financially ready. That word is legacy. Legacy, by definition, is a gift by will especially of money or other personal property; something transmitted by or received from an ancestor or predecessor, or from the past. Legacy, I believe, extends to more than financial, but also educational. It is a legacy of insight, knowledge, psychology, attitude, and life choices.

The catalyst for the question I first asked stems from a desire and goal for generations coming behind us to have something to remember us by; something that will be a benefit to them and their lives. However, to leave a legacy, you must first be willing to think beyond yourself; to want to give a gift to your loved ones that they will be able to reap many blessings from long after you have passed away.

All of the "greats" I previously mentioned created a lasting legacy for the generations that would follow after them, their sons and daughters and grandsons and granddaughters. But most importantly, these entrepreneurs understood the importance of financial readiness and preparing for their last days.

> *"He who is best prepared can best serve in his moment of inspiration."*
>
> *– Samuel Taylor Coleridge*

So, how important are the decisions we make about finances to our legacy? The short answer is: very important. The long answer is more detailed and has to do with decision-making. Consider this: Why do we wait to make decisions only when under pressure? An answer to this may be that until it's your problem, it's not your problem. There are problems that we are all sure to face. Therefore, the key is to know how to stop and make financial decisions today rather than when you're under pressure to make a decision. Now, no one can be fully prepared for everything that life will thrust upon them, but with financial strategies and preparation, and a model to follow, we can do the best we can to protect ourselves now, and our families once we're gone.

Laying the foundation

The path I chose to follow in my professional life was a deviation from my brothers. My grandfather was an eye doctor; my father is a doctor; my older brother is a doctor; my three younger brothers are doctors, and my son's a dentist. I know… pretty wild! Medicine was not for me, so I had to make a decision in college as to what I was going to do with my life. When I made the decision to go into business, that was not something anyone else in the family had ever done. Even though they're all successful business people, their business is medicine. (Healthcare is a benefit that society believes is worth taking care of, so there are billions of dollars provided for it. I was the odd man out because of my chosen career and had to work differently than they did to see any of my dollars.)

Prior to getting into the business that I'm in, I had worked at Radio Shack in college, selling stereos, and all things electronic. I worked at Albertson's stocking shelves at night. I also worked at the Holiday Inn, doing the night audit. After my second year of college, I took a year off because I didn't know what I wanted to with my life once I graduated. Was I going to study accounting, or marketing, or finance, or whatever? I couldn't decide so I took several months off, and worked from 11 PM 'til 2 PM, seven days a week, at three different jobs. I saved money and finished my Associate's degree at a community college. It gave me a firmer foundation, financially. I later returned to school at Florida State University to earn my Bachelor's degree and graduated in 1980.

Right before graduation, my father asked me if I wanted to get into the boating business with him. So I did. I was young and eager to see what we could do, so I dove right in. It was a way for my father to be able to get boating supplies for discounts, and have a business at the same time. The excitement for me was that I'd have a business, be living at home, and get paid $100 a week. A dream job, right? The reality of it was I'd also be working six days a week in a store that needed three -million dollars worth of inventory, and we only had $30,000 of inventory. It was a no-win. I quickly realized that it wasn't for me. We all have different endeavors that we can succeed at in life and some that we don't have the heart to succeed in. Unfortunately, the boating business was not the desired business I had in mind.

After I left boating business, I spent four months in Philadelphia becoming a paralegal for pension plans for ERISA: Employee Retirement Income Security Act. I worked in my future father-in-law's branch office. It wasn't the paralegal work I thought it would be; it was pension administration work. That was more in line with accounting, and it was not to my liking. After a year and a half I left that position and decided to branch out on my own. I needed to get sales experience, so I worked at night and on weekends, selling cable TV door-to-door for several months so that I could toughen my outer skin and get used to hearing the word "No."

During my door-to-door sales, I was also building up enough courage to be able to say to my then father-in- law that I was ready to be a life insurance agent, and ask him how much money he would give me.

When I approached my father-in-law about the money, his response was, "What do you mean, 'How much money are we going to give you?' If you're going to sell, that's how you're going to get your money." He asked me if I had thought about how long I would give myself to see if I could make it in the sales business. I thought maybe six months to a year. To my surprise, he told me ten days, maybe twenty days. We settled on 45 days. I couldn't afford to make long-distance phone calls from where I lived to where I wanted to work, so he let me use his phone to make long-distance calls from Miami to Naples, but then I started a nine-year commute. No one I knew in business was choosing to do this at that time. Every week, I drove to Fort Myers and Naples to work two days there to build up my business. In order to make appointments, I didn't start at the A's in the phonebook, I started at the Z's and worked my way up to the beginning of it, cold- calling every name I could in an effort to sell life insurance plans. I started at the Z's because I figured less people had gotten to them. And it worked!

In 1982, I got my insurance license. I sold a policy to a friend and then sold one to myself. This essentially summed up my "intangible" sales experience. Then in '84, I wanted to go out on my own. That's when I was able to sell life insurance and disability insurance. I started meeting physicians and people that made good incomes. The purpose of them purchasing life insurance was, God forbid, they died or got disabled, they needed to know what would happen with their families. Then in '86, I got my securities license for mutual funds, and after that a limited partnership license.

While I was building my business, I was learning about other people's businesses and what they were doing. The transition happened for me when years into being in life insurance sales I realized people didn't understand the products that I sold them, specifically life insurance and permanent insurance. I couldn't understand why somebody would buy life insurance as they got older. In fact, I didn't completely understand the value of it myself. It didn't completely make sense until I kept seeing people over and over again, and saw what some were doing that was successful, and what wasn't. When my kids got into elementary school, it became paramount for me to make sure they were knowledgeable about money. I started teaching kids after school cash-flow games. They called me "Mr. Money".

During college, I kept moving from one job to another because each job looked better than the next and so on. It paid more, or I got more from it. I would just leave one job to go to the other. While bouncing from job to job, I realized that there was always going to be something that looked better. Along the way, I learned that the grass I saw as always greener on the other side of the fence was because they were fertilizing. If I just fertilized my grass then it would be green. I applied that to my personal development, personal and professional, rather than thinking it was better to switch jobs. I knew that if I didn't quit and kept going, I would have to win in the end; I would have to be successful. One valuable lesson I did learn from the many sales jobs I had was that I didn't like selling tangible things; I liked selling ideas and concepts.

The course of my life steered me to choose the road less traveled when I decided to get into the insurance sales business. In doing so, traveling that road, I accepted the challenge and as the Robert Frost poem stated, "It has made all the difference."

Contemplating Your Legacy

My background in finance has given me a wealth of experience in not only understanding money but also understanding people. My goal is to organize, simplify, and dramatically improve my client's financial lives. And also maybe help them to think of ways where they could help others with their money. This begins by first thinking beyond yourself and valuing the importance of leaving a legacy.

I once had clients that were a group of seven doctors who needed disability insurance. I sold to them and made enough money to remain in the business another year. From there, I met another group of people and also sold them life insurance. I started seeing what people were doing with their money and how I had a direct influence on their decisions—negatively or positively. You see financial institutions don't want you to know how to work money. But I was determined to help them make good decisions.

There are little things that can be done to have a dramatic impact on our legacy. You must be consciously aware of how your life can make a difference in the lives of others. Ask yourself if you exist to solely consume things or to give back. I would say that it's less important to consume and more important to give back. The impact of your life on others lasts longer than your actual life. You're going to leave some sort of legacy, good or bad, but the quality of that legacy is highly dependent upon what you do **here and now**.

It is so vital that each and every individual take the time to stop and think deeply about his/her financial aspect and legacy as opposed to continuing through life blissfully ignorant until it's too late. Therefore, my purpose in writing this book is to cause you to pause, consider, and deeply contemplate what your legacy will be.

You may have been wondering why I chose the title *If I Should Wake Before I Die*, for my book. Well, there are many things we do out of sheer habit because we know it's beneficial for us. Things like exercising, or getting a check-up from the doctor, seeing a dentist, eating well, etc. However, being financially prepared does not often make it to this list of habits. This book's title is meant to stir you to action to immediately get financially prepared for your loved ones in the event you should die. I want you not to delay. Find a reputable financial planning expert who can assist you in getting started. You can begin small by first writing down the most crucial things in your life now, and what you want to happen to them in the event you pass away. This is not a difficult exercise and it doesn't need to be done every day. It's a process that you can start and immediately complete, then review it again in three or four years if something major happens in your life in those years.

The title of this book should cause you to value the importance of your life **now**. I want you to be awakened to what is in your best interest before you die. And I'm here to help you do it right for their first time so that you can have peace of mind and rest.

Imagine the kind of gift you can give to your loved ones; a gift that can only come from you. We all need to wake before we die. What does that mean? It means to be aware and awake to the reality that we all will have to pass away at some point in our lives, and must give a gift to our loved ones that only you can give.

It's time to figure out the financial and estate planning aspects of your life now…not later.

Q **How do you want people to remember you? What do you want your legacy to be?**

Chapter 1

Searching for Happiness with Money

It is not how much we have, but how much we enjoy, that makes happiness.

— Charles Spurgeon

We've all heard it before, that money makes you happy. Surely it does, right? In fact, we've seen happiness in the lives of wealthy celebrities like reality stars and singers; or CEOs and athletes. However, could happiness come from something else other than money? The answer is an unequivocal, yes! I propose we flip happiness on its head so that I can cause you to think differently, and think more, about what happiness means. Perhaps happiness is more about responsibility and not just about joy?

I believe that financial responsibility is a prerequisite to true happiness. Responsibility plays a significant role in happiness because being responsible means knowing what you can and can't do, while also understanding the financial steps you must do for your loved ones. You must make sure to act now so that you don't leave all sorts of financial problems for your family when you pass away.

Money isn't about relationships. The relationships are what bring you happiness, not the money. You must decide what is important to you: creating a lasting positive legacy with your money or being happy. Decide whether you want to be in a better place today than you were in yesterday—especially being in a better place relationally with your loved ones.

If Today Were your Last Day on Earth

Understanding that happiness is more about responsibility than about personal joy, I'd like you to ponder the following questions:

⦿ What would you do if today were your last day on Earth?

② Where would you go?

③ Who would you spend it with?

④ How would you spend your money?

⑤ How would you want to be remembered?

Living Life Without Regrets

Imagine living a life where every thoughtful decision you made about your future and your finances came without regrets. In the previous paragraph, you answered some questions about how you would spend your last days on Earth and how you would spend your money. Thinking deeply about how you would spend your last days should cause you to want to ensure that you have no regrets in your life leading up to that time. It should cause you to leave no stone unturned or words left unspoken, and that you leave your loved ones a sense of financial security that they can happily remember you by.

Consider this: a twenty-one-year-old begins working for a company. He lives at home and has no expenses, making a fifty thousand dollar salary. He could put away (save or invest) one hundred percent of everything he earns, and have a great rate of return with his boss matching it dollar-for-dollar. So if the total fifty thousand dollar salary went to taxes and withholding, and the balance of forty-five thousand went to his retirement plan, and he worked there for thirty years, he would have a substantial financial cushion to aid him in his financial preparedness for himself and generations after him. This is an ideal scenario for building wealth and having an opportunity to live a life with no regrets as a result of financial preparedness. If everything worked out great he'd have a lot of money.

But let's consider a different outcome for this scenario. What happens if along the way this twenty-one-year-old loses his job, or gets sick, or has an increase in expenses, or takes a different job? What I am trying to get at is that anything that you would spend from your savings can begin to dwindle once you have other expected or unexpected expenses. He will have to reduce what he has accumulated from that forty-five thousand dollars he has in his savings. It's important to understand how money flows than where it is saved. (This also ties into understanding term life insurance versus permanent life insurance. We will talk more about this in a later chapter.)

People go about accumulating wealth in a certain way thinking that's how you do it because that's what they've been taught to do—how they've been trained to think. Being responsible with your money and long-term planning is not just about accumulating wealth; it's about getting more than one use out of your money. It's about protecting it during plentiful times and lean times.

When I meet with clients to discuss how they should save or put their money into something that is long-term, I don't say to them, "Well, let's plan on you having 'X' amount at retirement". Instead I say, "Let's do the most efficient method with your money today, and we'll do that every time we get together to make sure you have the most efficient use of your money." In the end, we'll get what we get. Sometimes it turns out to be more than what you plan on because you're not trying to get to some made up point. That's how the economy works as well. It's economics or searching for limited resources to be the most efficient and to get the most. If you remember anything, remember this: You must be aware of your finances; don't be afraid to ask questions. And don't sabotage your happiness by being financially unaware and irresponsible.

The Importance of Setting Goals

Goal setting has been something that people have been doing for quite a long time. Whether it's a short-term goal or a long-term goal, there is always something that we want to reach for or strive to complete or improve upon in our lives. Goal setting is an action shared by many. For example, this year has birthed many New Year's resolution goals: weight loss, investing, travel, living healthier, earning a degree, etc. Unfortunately, goals often get set and they often don't get accomplished. According to the University of Scranton's research, just 8% of people who set long-term goals actually achieve them. Although this statistic may sound grim, this same research states that people who explicitly make resolutions are ten times more likely to attain their goals than people who don't explicitly make long-term resolutions because of the simple act of taking that first step to set a goal.

Setting goals is first a mental process before it springs into action. This mental process begins with the words you speak to, and over, yourself. What words do you speak to yourself? Are they encouraging, challenging, motivating words, or are they words that you've gotten used to hearing that tear you down and discourage your desire for success? What words are you allowing to penetrate your mind in order to challenge you in your goal setting? Start with reading challenging personal development books. Then move on to people. Carefully choose whom you will surround yourself with—people that will cause you to do and be more, and to think beyond yourself. Goal setting enables you to keep yourself grounded and focused on the goals you've set when everything else seems like it's falling apart.

Happiness is not a goal; it should be a state of being. Financial responsibility is a goal. Happiness will also come along because you haven't focused on the pie in the sky, but focused instead on practical measures that will bring lasting joy.

Q **What goals have you set for your life? Short-term and long-term?**

Chapter 2

Financial Fitness

Financial freedom is available to those who learn about it and work for it.

— Robert Kiyosaki

In this chapter, I'd like to focus on **you** and **your thoughts** regarding money. My goal is for you to take an introspective look at your finances. Let's begin with a few questions:

- What are your first memories of money?

_____

_____

_____

_____

_____

_____

_____

How has that first impression influenced how you think of money now?

_____

_____

_____

_____

_____

How you viewed money growing up as a child directly affects how you view, and use, money now as an adult. The way our parents interacted with money has taught us to be slaves to our money, anxiously waiting on the next paycheck to pay our bills or depending on a 30-year stint at a company to get our financial payout to retire on. Or, our parents' interaction with money has taught us to look at money as a tool to not only help us to pay the bills, but to also help us plan for the future.

Savers or Spenders

The Savers I've worked with often explain that their financial traits were taught to them as a child from a parent or grandparent. Those money lessons stuck with them and directly influenced how they think about money and practice financial planning today. I believe those valuable money lessons are missing today—mainly because of the vast material items we want and think we need to purchase immediately, making it difficult to stop spending. There are so many people and things after our money that it's almost impossible to set any of it aside for saving. There are basic needs for children and family, then government taxes, or the latest and greatest products on the market that we absolutely need to make our lives better and help us work smarter. What you want now can overpower any desire you have to save up for something else. This is the age of: *I want it now and I don't want to wait.*

There are so many demands today on our money. Demands like: car payments, mortgages, vacation packages, new shoes for the kids, birthday presents for grandchildren, college tuition, etc. When my children were younger, I spent a lot of money providing for them.

Often, it is much easier to satisfy an immediate need or want today than to delay gratification for tomorrow. However, what if you could get more than one use out of your money? Would you agree to it? It is actually much easier to put your money somewhere for it to grow and produce multiple benefits for you today and in the future. This is how Spenders transition to Savers, and Savers multiply their benefits.

Consider this analogy: As a kid, I played two well-known board games. One was called Checkers, and the other was Chess. Many people would agree with me that it is much easier to play Checkers than it is to play Chess. The concept of money can be learned while playing both Chess than Checkers—one more than the other. Each game uses the same game board; each has a goal of capturing their opponent. However, the game of Chess has multiple players, each with their own set of rules. Both games are offensive and defensive. To be a good Saver, you must understand the offensive and the defensive position of your dollars. With both games, just as in life, your opponent is after you so being strategic is critical.

Strategy is what will make the difference. You must strategize and take responsibility for how you will live financially now and how your family will live financially after you have passed away.

Running up the Rates

Most people believe that getting the greatest rate of return is the number one goal that they should be doing with their money. While it's important to get a good rate of return, what's much more important is stopping the losses and recovering losses of money. When you think about how much money we pay for the various insurances: car, homeowners, umbrella, disability, and health insurance premiums. When you add that up over 40 or 50 years, you're in the millions of dollars. All that money is gone. Are there ways you can help get some of that back? What other decisions are we doing that are hurting us financially? Take, for instance, that all your money is in a qualified plan and you're going to retire. You retire the following year, and the President raises the income taxes. You may end up paying more money getting your money out of your retirement plan in taxes than you did if you had taken it when you were working. If that's the only place you have money and the taxes are higher, it's pretty hard to get away from not paying the higher taxes. You should have other options or another strategy in place in order to offset the higher taxes.

One analogy that comes to mind to explain this scenario is climbing a ladder as an image of trying to amass wealth, whether for college or retirement. You climb up the ladder and then you realize that it's actually the ladder for a diving board and now you have to jump into the swimming pool and start all over again because you gave all your money to complete a college degree or you gave it all to the government. Since you didn't strategize or financially plan properly, now you're going to have to start all over again. The problem is that you end up starting all over when you're ten years older. You have that much less time now to accumulate money.

Everyone is born with something called an exponential curve and the exponential curve says if you start with a little bit of money and continue to add money, as time goes on and the years go buy and you invest it, it will start to increase. But the curve needs time to grow.

Let's look at some numbers. If you put $1,000 a year away into a college fund at age 1 or 0, after 10 years, you would've put $10,000 in. Assuming you'd had earned some rate of return, it's now worth, just say, $13,500. The exponential curve exploding growth doesn't happen until after 20 years. At 18 just when you're about to get that now $20,000 you've put in that's maybe grown to $40,000. That $40,000 then goes to a college and you take that $40,000 off your model and give it to the school. Who would be better off? The person that did that or the person that said I'm not going to college? Leave the money where it is and let's see what it grows to over the next 40 years. That's how you find out how much college costs. College costs $40,000 plus other earnings on that $40,000 that you lost. If you do a fast calculation, we're talking hundreds of thousands of dollars.

That's why when it's important to evaluate the cost of school and what it costs to the earning potential of that degree. Many people have gone to school and borrowed money to get degrees, then the likelihood of their being able to pay their loans back was slim and difficult. This is why it is important to evaluate whether something economically makes sense. Is it good to have an education, but at what cost?

In finances, there's a cost to every decision even if you don't spend the money. The truth is, even when you think you don't spend the money, you do. It'll cost both sides. Opportunity costs are not spoken about much, but they certainly are a part of economics – a huge part.

There is a rule in finance called the 28%-36% Rule. I believe this rule is what got the country in trouble in 2008 with the real estate crash. These numbers are a gauge for the percentage of money that should be spent on large expenses, like the purchase of a home or a car. Twenty-eight percent is the maximum amount of mortgage, interest, taxes, and insurance you should spend of your gross income on your home. If you have a car, the maximum amount of your car payments should be 36% of your gross income. What happens is it means your housing shouldn't cost you more than 28% of your gross income and all your other debts combined shouldn't exceed another 8%. This is a traditional underwriting rule for banking and loaning money. If you go too high in those numbers, there's going to be a problem.

The real-estate crisis and crash occurred because people were able to borrow money on earnings they didn't even have to purchase real estate. This caused all the traditional numbers to flip upside down, and the market couldn't continue the charade any longer. The 2008 real estate crisis is one of the things economists still look at today as an example of what *not* to do.

We are all part of a giant economy. When someone is financially fit, they're participating in this giant economy and hopefully giving back to help others. Why be financially fit? It's a better and healthier way to live.

Building Money Strength

During the process of exercising or focused and rigorous activity, there is a certain calmness and comfort that athlete possesses. This is because they are in control, and this control feels good. This same perspective applies to money. When you're in control of your money, you have a sense of comfort and confidence just like you do if you're working out. It can be likened as well to being in a faith-based environment. Financial fitness relates to physical fitness and spiritual fitness.

I taught a financial course to students in grade 2nd-8th. I titled it *Financial Fitness 4 Life*. For this course, I spend Wednesday afternoons at St. Francis Elementary School in my city playing financial games with these students. I had four games going on at once. There were different versions of this Cash Flow game, but it was teaching everything that can happen in life, but in the game it happened very quickly. During the game, you could have gotten a job, lost your job, had a flat tire, and had to buy a new tire, and got married, and had children, all in one hour. A lot would happen fast. You had a job, you had income, you had expenses, and the kids learned it didn't take the highest earning person to win the game; it took the person that was managing their cash flow the best to ensure that they were not spending more than they made.

Take care of your wealth. These games taught them about the value of money, the rate of return when you save and invest, and how to let your money work for your benefit instead of only working for money. I also taught them about income, expenses, taxes, insurance, unexpected expenses, and much more. I didn't want them to think of it as a boring math class that they would eventually hate. Rather, I wanted it to be a class on life lessons.

They gave me the moniker of "The Moneyman." I taught the course for two hours during a four week time period to twenty-four kids. I also had a few teachers visit my class who saw the model I used and expressed an interest in seeing themselves on the model. The idea of the game was to teach that your money could eventually work and provide enough income for you so you didn't have to work. I did it as a way to give back—to help remove the fear of money from their minds. I especially did it to provide insight into how people deal with money and the issues surrounding financial preparedness.

Many of the students I once taught this course are now well out of college. I taught this course because I wanted kids to understand money. They represent the next generation, and this next generation must be wise about money—its value and its use.

Did you know that seventy percent of the population goes to bed worrying about money? Why does this happen? Because getting your finances in control is critical to your personal and professional success, your health, your stability, and your peace of mind. Just as you take care of yourself physically, you must also take care of your wealth.

Retirement is not an end but a beginning of your life. There are so many complexities of life that are critical, and being financially prepared and fit is definitely one of them.

Chapter 3

Complete Your Estate Plan

"An estate plan spells out how you want your life's work to be remembered."

— Paul Harris

What is an Estate Plan?

An estate plan is all the legal papers you execute expressing your last wishes (your last will and testament) for everything you personally own, your personal items, jewelry, etc. to your home, to charities. It states what you want to happen after you pass away.

An estate plan helps to make things as seamless as possible. Generally, people don't think they're going to pass away and therefore don't want to think about it. So, this results in absolutely no planning or preparation ahead for when it does happen. It all comes down to responsibility... everyone's responsibility. We must all plan and prepare for our future, especially because we don't want to. What is your responsibility? How do you want to be remembered?

Everyone essentially has an estate plan, because if you die without a will the state takes over the distribution of your possessions. And therefore the state in which you reside becomes the overseers of your estate plan. However, the way your possessions are distributed by the state will quite possibly be in a way that you would not approve of. In essence, you do not want the state to be responsible for relegating your assets and your needs. If you pass away without an estate plan the government creates one for you called intestacy—that's dying without a will, where none of your wishes have been written down. The state spells it out. However, this may not be what you'd want had you made certain arrangements within your estate plan. It's what the government says will happen because you don't have a will. An estate plan covers all these things. There are several documents that go into an estate plan. These documents include a will, along with a durable power of attorney, designating a health surrogate, a prenuptial agreement, a living will, computer passwords, and more. These documents should be looked at every four years, unless something big changes in your life before four years, in order for them to be kept up-to-date and reviewed in alignment with the current laws on estate planning. These laws can—and often do—change.

I'll share an example of this with you. Do you remember the story of Terry Schiavo? Terry Schiavo was a young married woman who had been placed on a feeding tube and pronounced brain dead after a cardiac arrest. Her parents wanted her to be kept alive, but her husband wanted to take her off of life support in order to end his wife's suffering. Her parents, however, couldn't let her go. So they brought it to court and had a very public legal battle. They fought for their daughter, but the court made the decision fifteen years later that their daughter would not want to live with machines keeping her alive. So, the family had to pull the plug.

Having a document like a living will assists in having situations like these spelled out specifically for medical personnel and family members. The revised one now allows you to initial areas asking direct questions like: give patient water, give patient pain medicine, do you give food, and all these different things that you would say yes or no to. These details help the hospital system or nursing home needs know exactly what to do for their patients.

Another similar situation was that of the singer/songwriter Prince. He passed away last year and did not have a will. His estate is estimated to be worth millions of dollars. He also has extended family members who are now fighting for his money. One must consider that somewhere along the way someone could have advised him to create a will. Being a celebrity, I'm sure he had many knowledgeable people around him who could have told him about the importance of having a will. Now, as a result of *not* having a will his millions were given to the government for them to determine how it would be dispersed, and to the legal fees for the family members fighting the court system for his millions. What a waste. Not to mention that perhaps the relationships of those siblings won't improve with the fighting that will take place. The repercussions of it will go on for years. The same thing happened with James Brown and Elvis Presley whose estates lost money in fees and costs because they didn't have wills. Therefore, this is why estate planning is so important, especially because it relieves the burden that can be put on family members to make decisions about you if a tragic incident occurs or if you are in your final days. An estate plan is systematized at making your life and the lives of your loved ones easier.

Estate planning is so important to me that I even do it with my own children. When they turned eighteen, I took them to an estate-planning attorney and had a will done for them. As much as could, I made sure that every possible need was covered in their wills at the time. They didn't have any assets, so I didn't create a trust, but healthcare, durable power, the will, everything. Why? Well, they were eighteen and of age at the time. They have their own rights, but if they needed my help with healthcare, I needed some way to prove that it was okay for HIPAA, for example, to allow the doctors to contact me. Or if I needed to get into their apartment because something was wrong with them, I would have the proper legal documents to prove that I had this power. I wanted to make sure I had these sorts of documents. Thank God I never had to use it. However, it was important for me knowing what could happen without it, so I wanted to make sure they had it.

Decision Making

When life planning, you always need to be looking ahead, as well as enjoying the present. Be aware of where you are in your life and how you're feeling about your situation. It's being content with where you are. When you start to worry about something, you know it's because you're living in the future or if you're saying things like, "I could've, should've, etc.", then you're in the past. Well, I've got to think it's a battle for everyone to stay in the present.

This may seem inconsequential, but when it comes to legal documents needed for estate planning, it is important that you sign each and every document so that there are no errors or miscommunication once you pass away. Don't go online, print something and sign it, thinking that an online document will suffice. It's all about the mechanics of making sure that you take care of the formality with those documents and get them all signed. Be sure that the signing takes place in front of a notary and with two other witnesses. In some cases, there are some attorneys that will have you initial every page of all the documents, acknowledging that you saw it and read it.

When making plans regarding your estate once you die, you must also be aware of the estate planning laws regarding your particular state. For example, in my state of Florida, some people may have a summer home here and a winter home elsewhere, or vice versa. Owning these two properties could affect your estate planning. In Florida, there is no state income tax but the state where your winter home resides could have a state income tax. When someone dies and they have residency in both places, the burden will be on the family to prove that their parents did in fact live in one state more than the other, which would make it their home state. There are a number of ways to prove this. First, it can be done by getting a driver's license, and in this example it would be a Florida driver's license. Then having an attorney you've met with in Florida, showing proof of address with any mail, registering to vote in said state, that you don't leave legal stuff just for up north that you do, where you vote up there. It's important that you go through the necessary steps, and make sure that you domicile where you are. If somebody had to prove you actually lived here and this is your permanent home, could they do it?

An estate plan provides peace of mind for both the individual and their family. The decisions they want executed will be put into effect the way they intend it to when they pass away. You don't want to leave your family with the burden of deciding your estate because you didn't take the time to organize or plan. In truth, only you are responsible for your life and thus, your estate planning. Estate planning is something you must be motivated to do. Though it is not a task you may be excited about jumping into, estate planning is a task worth doing.

Q **Does an estate plan fit your personal financial situation?**

Q **What decisions can you make now regarding your estate plan?**

Chapter 4

Protection from Life's Risks

"March on. Do not tarry. To go forward is to move toward perfection. March on, and fear not the thorns, or the sharp stones on life's path."

— Khalil Gibran

To be a responsible adult in today's society you must insure yourself properly, and there's pretty much an insurance policy for almost any thing and every need. Any need you have, or can think of having in the future, has a possible insurance policy attached to it. Think about this: if an event happened, and you could buy insurance the day after the event, what type of insurance would you choose to buy? Typically people buy insurance for what they think they need versus what they would actually want. In the past, I've asked clients this: *What if you were in a car accident and didn't have insurance for your car, but could go back in time just one day before that event and get it, how much insurance would you get?*

Whenever this question was posed, their response was always the same: they would get as much as they possibly could. However, people never get what they think they'd need. Many people are underinsured—for everything. People never actually get what they need when it comes to insurance. It's normally the big things that people are underinsured for. When you are underinsured it could result in your being at a financial loss, i.e.: a homeowner's insurance. Being underinsured is not a game that you can win.

There's an Insurance for That

Insurance comes in a variety of forms. There is car insurance, appliance insurance, and home or renter's insurance, just to name a few. There are policies known as umbrella policies that go over top your car and your homeowner's policy, stipulating that if you exceed those insurance amounts, the umbrella policy covers you for an additional one million dollars or more. I've even seen them into the tens of millions of dollars. Let's extend it further and talk about insuring your ability to earn an income. You can't ensure that you're always going to have a job, but if there comes a time where for some reason you cannot work, this type of insurance will prove to be a benefit to you and your family. **Insuring your income** proves to be a necessity because when you can't work for a certain amount of time, possibly years, you will eventually run out of money in your checking and savings accounts. Therefore, this is an insurance that will pay out to you an amount matching your income.

There are different ways that you can insure your income. However, in order to understand the value and reap the benefits of insuring your income, you must ask yourself these kind of questions: How long are you going to be disabled? How much do you need to live on per month? This is something that you must deeply think about, especially so for those who own their own businesses and have employees to pay or for those who are the sole breadwinners in their home. Moreover, consider a scenario where you can no longer work. Wouldn't you want to get what you needed or as much as you could get from your employer or insurance company?

There are particular policies for income insurance that will cover you from the moment you sign the paperwork for one week, six weeks, or thirteen weeks. Then, there is short-term disability (STD) that covers you for up to 26 weeks. Then there's long-term disability insurance that covers you for five years or up to age 65. And finally, there are some older policies that will cover you for your lifetime. (There are also options for situations where you can only work part time.) These are all called residual benefits. Also, what about inflation—the expansion or increase of currency? If you're disabled for several years, you may need your benefit to increase with inflation.

What I find is the younger someone is, the more important it is for him/her to have that inflation protection built in. There are also options in the future where you can guarantee your ability to buy additional coverage without any health questions. People think premium is what buys insurance. In fact, what actually buys insurance, is your good health. Usually, people think that it's the premium that indicates the value of the insurance, making it worthwhile to buy it. Obviously, you need the premium, but it's your good health that allows you to get the insurance in the first place. Let's unpack this even more.

Long-term care is probably the most recognizable need among retirees, or those close to retirement age. People are in need of long-term care, and there is insurance for that need as well. It seems to be something that catches a lot of people's attention because everyone's known of someone that has needed long-term care. The cost of this kind of care is hundreds of dollars a day, and dependent on how long someone needs it. In total, it runs into the hundreds of thousands of dollars. I've found that in some cases long-term care insurance makes sense, and in others it doesn't make sense based on other assets held by the individual.

A huge benefit that we all now are required to have is **health insurance.** And it doesn't have a limit of how much they'll pay out—maybe a million or five million. The benefit is unlimited, which obviously transfers the risk to the insurance company. We're seeing premiums jump so high that I project in the not too distant future that the cost of health insurance is going to be higher than what a medium salary is today. Something has to be done politically in an effort to control the cost.

Life insurance, where, again, if you knew you were going to die tomorrow and you could get the insurance today, how much would someone get? An adult decision is, well in advance of that event just like any insurance, is what would happen if this loss occurred? What would be ideal for you? In making that decision, when I'm consulting with clients, we run through exercises to show what happens with inflation, college costs, wedding costs, etc. One needs to ask themselves: What do I want for my family? What do I want for my charities? Is there anyone I want to benefit, or any organization? There are unlimited uses for it, and unlimited directions of where it can go.

If there were ever an insurance I would not recommend purchasing it would be identity protection insurance. This is a type of insurance most people should not buy. There are others as well: dental insurance and technology insurance (iPhones, cameras, etc.) What is a risk to one person may not be a risk to another person, so something like insurance on your iPhone may not be important to you, but to the foreman on a construction site who often drops his cell phone on the ground, it may be very important. Sometimes purchasing something like cell phone insurance or insurance for a new camera may be based on the person's income or emotional connection to the item.

You must weigh the cost for yourself and your lifestyle.

Some insurance policies are designed to be prepayments or savings plans, but the benefits of these types of insurance policies are limited. Insurance policies have changed because society has changed; families have changed. People don't live close to family members anymore. Most times the responsibility to take care of "mom" falls on the daughter—on women.

Social Security

There's also Social Security, which people often forget about. Originally, it was set up as old age benefit for retirement, but it also provides widow benefit, it provides for children and if a parent passes away, and it provides a benefit for disability if someone's working and goes out on disability. It's a form of insurance that we all pay for in our paycheck, and they've increased the amount of income you earn to be taxed. So they've raised millions more dollars to keep it funded, which I believe will continued to be done. I believe they are going to keep extending the age at which you can retire at full retirement age. It used to be 65 but now it's gone up to age sixty-seven. I project that eventually it's going to go out to age seventy.

Social Security is an important consideration for your life, but it was never intended to be the whole plan for retirement. Moreover, by the time you begin collecting your Social Security, it doesn't leave much time for an actual retirement where you still have energy and useful vitality to be able to go and do everything you dreamed of in retirement. A 59-year-old may think about how long they are going to work and what their energy level will be like when they're 70 and how much energy am I going to have? What's happening is, the economy is requiring most households to have two people working to afford to live and get what they want, but it's working against them to accumulate money. Less than 1% of the population has a million dollars or more at age 65. An overwhelming majority of the population has very minimal saved for retirement. The reason they're extending it out is because people are living so much longer than they used to. When they first set it up, people at 65 usually were passed away within five years.

My parents are 88 and 86, and my father was disabled in his early mid-60's. I recently asked him when he began receiving his Social Security. He said he was age 63. Well now he's been on Social Security for 25 years, and there's a 0.3% increase this year in benefits. Now the other story is, someone who dies at 67, they didn't get Social Security but two years. You know there's going to be some that get it for a long time, some that don't. He also at 88, just had a quadruple bypass, now his heart is as young as a 50-year-old, and the risk was worth it for him. He's still talking and moving around and joking and he wants to be alive. He's even talking about working again. A 70-year-old is now more like a 50-year-old because their lifestyle is more active today because of health care and medicine, which leads to better health.

As we've all seen, the government is very involved in paying benefits that people have contributed to. Some people will contribute obviously more, and Social Security was set up as one of the sources of retirement, but for a lot it's the only one. It's supposed to be Social Security and your personal savings, along with your employer's retirement plan. Social Security is a lifetime of payments so to gain the most out of Social Security you'd want to be in the best of health and wait until age 70 to get the largest monthly payment with the potential to maximize your lifetime benefits.

Social Security retirement benefits are considered a pension benefit. The formula pays out more per month the later you start receiving the benefit. There is no sole right decision for everyone. Things like health, family history, assets, and income, all play a part. The one guarantee is that only after you pass away will you know when you should have started taking your Social Security benefits. And another guarantee is that your spouse will begin receiving your benefits after you pass away.

Many people are choosing to take Social Security as soon as they can at age 62 and they're potentially losing. They're losing 30% of their monthly benefits by taking it early, instead of waiting and taking it later around ages 65 or 66. Social Security has a very specific calculator at sss.gov that assesses your estimated benefits from age 62 to age 70. The formula is actuarially based over millions of people's life expectancies. So to say someone always loses by taking the Social Security benefits at 62 would depend on how long they live and if they have a beneficiary whose benefit will be based on their benefit. If your benefit as the wage earner is 1,800 at age 65 and $1,500 at age

62 the entire benefit isn't known until the last payment is made to the surviving spouse.

There are arguments for and against why you should take Social Security benefits early and why you should take them later. The only example that I bring up is when should my father have taken it? Knowing that he could have been on it so many years, obviously the bigger the monthly check, the more he would have gotten, but he'd have to wait until he was older to get it. You don't know what was the right way until after you're gone but people, because of the country and the way financial education is, and people's understanding and/or inability to get ahold of some of their money before it's gone, haven't been able to accumulate enough so that they have to take Social Security as soon as they can, to live. Social Security is the second to the last, as far as insurance protection. The next two don't have anything to do with "insurance" but they do play a huge role when it comes to protecting yourself through things like: having an estate plan, be it wills, power of attorney, who's going to take care of the kids.

You must also always make sure to audit your Social Security statements. Through the use of the Internet it is now very easy to access a wealth of information online. For example, anyone can register an account online at SSA.gov/my account. Once on the site, you will create an account, password and sign on for your Social Security. You can go in and see if what you've earned has been reported properly on your W2 to the Social Security Administration. It tells you what your benefit's going to be when you hit 65 or for you it's going to be 67, if you were disabled, what you get. It's going to show if you were married and had children, what the family benefit could be. You might not know this, but they used to mail it to everyone every year. They've since stopped that. Now they started mailing it just if you're 60 or older. If there's a mistake, you only have three years to correct it.

To figure out your retirement benefit, they take the top 35 years of earnings to figure out what your maximum Social Security benefit is. Do your own research and find out for yourself what's is going on with your Social Security account.

To Protect and Serve

I believe that most people, if given the choice, would want to get as much as they could after a loss that has occurred in their family. Just like gambling, if you knew your bet was going to win beforehand, you would put as much money as possible on it. This concept could apply to everything in life: knowing ahead of time that you were going to be successful and win, would give you newfound confidence that you could not fail. So the question becomes, what's realistic with your insurance planning? Do we cover every loss, or just the potentially large losses? If we're going to get coverage, we must make each dollar get the best overall use.

The key difference between this and gambling is in gambling you never know for sure if you're going to win the next roll of the wheel or flip of the card, but with permanent life insurance you know you are eventually going to "win" because nobody lives forever. Believe it or not, it is the one insurance you can buy that you can guarantee will pay. It's the only one, and it shouldn't be lumped into "all the other insurance" because your car insurance, your homeowner's, your disability, your long-term care, and your term insurance may not pay a benefit if you don't have a loss. You will only receive a payment if you have permanent coverage. That means that someone's insured for half a million dollars today, and then thirty years from now, inflation's taken its toll on that half a million. When they die, they know that there's going to be half a million dollars paid. I believe that is a huge economic win for that insured, as well as their family.

They know something is definitely going to happen. The person knows two things: they're going to pass, and they also know that the insurance is going to pay. I don't know of anything insurance-wise that can give someone more financial peace of mind knowing they have that. The question is, how do we make it part of their overall planning so that they have it when they die, and that they have it paid for like all the other insurances, and not lose it before they go. Because if they lose it, it's millions of dollars lost. Let's say someone enters an agent's office and they are a blank slate; they don't have any insurance other than what's required by law. What sort of hierarchy of insurance needs do you think the agent would provide them—telling them what insurance to purchase first, second, or third, and also what amounts? Would the agent recommend that they get a little bit each: a little bit of life insurance, a little bit of home owner's insurance, a little bit of car insurance, and then try to increase over time in each of those areas? Or should they start with a lot of life insurance and not as much of the other kinds of insurance? Would it all even make sense? What would be your general approach to organizing?

Organizing these different kinds of insurance in terms of importance is absolutely paramount. Think of it as if you were playing chess, and you have these different players on the board that represents the different insurances. When it comes to insurance, you take risks with the deductibles and the amount of coverage you purchase. The game of chess is also about taking risks when comparing losing a pawn to having to pay a $500 deductible for an auto repair. The real way to play the game is playing offensively and defensively with your chess pieces just like you are with your driving. You want to protect your pieces in chess, but it's not by insurance. Only in your financial life can you get insurance to protect your assets.

You can't get a car without car insurance, but you can decide how little or how much insurance you want. You don't have to have renter's insurance, but if you have a mortgage on your house, you have to have homeowner's, and they're going to tell you the minimum you have to have. If you have assets and savings, or as you said, this person, they don't have anything. If they don't have any assets, then maybe the umbrella policy isn't important right now. If someone doesn't have a job and they can't work, is disability insurance important for them to have? Should it be short-term or should it be catastrophic for long term? If this person has a health insurance claim, should they have a high premium with low out-of-pocket costs or should they have a low premium, but high out-of-pocket costs? These are worthwhile questions to consider when it comes to the type of insurance that is suitable for you and your family.

Wills and trusts, and other estate planning documents, aren't "insurance products." In fact, they are your decision on how you want your Personal Representative to act after you're gone. Moreover, life insurance isn't just like any other insurance. What amounts would we want to leave for our beneficiaries when we die? Would it be five times, ten times, or 15 times your earnings? Excellent health and premiums are what allow you to purchase life insurance. So consider this: does it make sense for a young person just beginning their career to have life insurance? I leave that up to my clients when I'm talking with them. I say, "What we're trying to do is build a moat around your future wealth." Most people have a minimal amount of life insurance. The average amount is under $200,000 for a man and a $140,000 for a woman. Honestly, that isn't a very deep moat, and depending on the value of their incomes, this amount will not last that long. When considering the dollar amount for life insurance, you must question your goals and ask yourself what exactly you are trying to insure. Do you need just enough, a lump sum, to provide income for your family to live and survive? Do you want to have enough money to give a gift for charity? Or maybe you would rather have enough more to provide not merely a lump sum for your family, but rather a stream of payments for your spouse and children. Do you have enough money to set aside to pay for college? The decisions that you have to make specifically for your life, and your family, are unique to you and they should be treated as such.

All those things are evaluated in client discussions, just like you'd have with a patient about their health. I'm going to recommend that every one of these be evaluated, and decisions come up with each component to make the client feel the most comfortable they can. What kind they get, the amount they get, it's their decision, but it's overall done with, what's future planning? What's going to happen in the future? If we look out five years, ten years, what else do we need to be doing?

There's not a one-size-fits-all list or checklist that you can go down and say, "Okay, $500,000 in life insurance, $100,000 in disability insurance..." and then be done. Rather, you need someone who's knowledgeable to create a personalized plan for you. It won't be cookie cutter. Also, people have beliefs, strong, emotional beliefs about things from their own experiences. They may think something are much more important than something else, and obviously that's what we're going to focus on. However, there's a level of education that goes along with it too, because, like I said, it's individualized. One person can't say, "Well, if that's what they did, that's what I should do." That's a bandwagon mentality; and certainly not the way you want to purchase or organize your insurance or financial life.

What are we buying this protection for, any kind of protection? What is it for? In a car, it's pretty obvious; it's for a car. If it's a house, it's on a house. If you're disabled, you know what that's for. What are we trying to protect? It's our standard of living that we have at the time it happens. That would mean there's other money somewhere else. You have a mortgage payment, a car payment, other assets, retirement account that you don't want to have to invade before you were planning on using it. You don't want to have to use your retirement account when you're 40 years old because you didn't have the proper protection because you'll need the retirement account when you retire to save what you've already accumulated. You can protect what you've accumulated and allow yourself to continue to grow it so that you won't become impoverished.

Adults have responsibility. One of the challenges I face in my line of work is getting people to complete their will. It's something that needs to be done, but unfortunately most people put it off because they just don't want to talk about it or deal with it. Perhaps it's a fear of the inevitability that lies ahead –death. But, the truth is that it's not about you; it's about responsibility. If these events happen, how do you want it to be? Generally, the character of a person is that they want to do the right thing. People want to do the right thing. It's just they don't know what it is all the time and what direction to go in.

Working with people to get their wishes after death all written down –on paper—can take some gentle prodding.

I think probably one of the things I enjoy the most is that most people aren't going to die early; most people aren't going to get disabled; most people aren't going to, hopefully, have a car accident, have a house fire, and all those things; so, there's time to review. I don't approach any client with, "Next time we get together, we'll review to make this better." I want to leave them each time with the thought that we've got it the best it can be right now. Can we tweak it and make improvements? Yes, but we better make our lives the best it can be now because the risks are out there.

If you don't have that catastrophic protection and something happens at 40, then you have to dip into your retirement account, and then 25 years down the road when you're 65, wanting to use that money to retire, well now it's not there anymore, because you had to use it, and so this whole system is only as strong as the weakest link in the chain. Yeah, that's obviously a cliché, but the right one. I'm trying to think that it's a defense. Does the moat around your castle have holes in it? From my experience, there *are* holes and you do not even know it. Where are the holes? How fast are they draining? How do we plug them? There's a potential problem, and I like to say, "You want to protect yourself with that moat and then you want to put things in that moat that add even more protection."

There are other types of coverage you need to know about. There's car, home, renters, umbrella policy, liability policy, disability, long-term care, and short-term disability. There's health insurance; dental insurance; and vision insurance. There are also voluntary benefits that you can get as well, like cancer insurance or hospital insurance. For example, if you go in the hospital, they'll pay you so much per day. Like I said at the very beginning, there's almost insurance for almost anything that can happen to someone, and I look at insurance as something to cover the big events first, not the little things. Unfortunately, some of the little things can sabotage your personal finances, depending on where someone is in their life it can sabotage their financial setup. At different times, those policies may make sense where you are but as you build your wealth. It's just like the deductible on your car. If you have a $600 collision, do you submit a claim if you have a $500 deductible, or do you say to yourself, "I'll take the first $1,000 of risk on my car insurance, because I'm not going to submit a claim if it's under $1,000 otherwise my premium is going to go up." The planning is if the worst happens, we've got the best plan. If something less than the worst happens, you've still got yourself covered.

Insure your home and personal property for its full replacement value. Why do you recommend that and what is the alternative that some people might do? Less than full replacement value? I went through Hurricane Andrew and my house had a hole blown through the roof, windows broken, water in it. The easy comparison is I had an eight-year old bed. I had replacement value. They did not make me buy an eight-year old bed. They allowed and paid me to buy a brand new bed for replacement value. While my bed I had was probably worth whatever an eight-year old bed was worth, I had the money, because on my policy it was replacement value, to buy a new bed. We had stereo equipment, computer equipment, or furniture. All that furniture was used, we'd lived in it, on it, used it. They didn't make me go out and buy used furniture. The policy covered replacement value.

Here's an example. If you had a $200,000 house and you insured it for $100,000, and a hurricane took it away. You have replacement value on the house, but you insured it for half of what it was worth. They're only going to pay you up to half of what you lost. There's two parts to this replacement value. One is you have to have it adequately insured at $200,000, and have replacement value on it. Flood insurance does not cover replacement value, but your homeowner's and renter's insurance does. If someone has their house paid off, they may think they don't' need to have insurance, but if they lost their house, they'd certainly want it insured for the most it could be.

There are some policies that you need a high deductible for, like auto insurance. Now, you may be wondering why I recommend a high deductible as opposed to a low deductible? The first reason is because the premium would be lower. The second is if you do have a claim, hopefully you have money in an emergency account to cover the deductible. If you have a $1,000 deductible on your car, and you have that $600 accident, you're going to not submit a claim, you're going to perhaps pay for it from your emergency money. That money that you saved on your premium could allow you to get full replacement cost. What I find is, I find people with maybe $100 or $250 deductible on their car insurance and they don't carry an umbrella policy. We are able to make adjustments where they end up without any additional dollars out of their pocket, having an additional coverage.

Many thousand dollars of additional coverage is going to be more valuable than having a deductible that's only $100 instead of $500 or $1000.

There are many types of policies, from term insurance, to whole life, to universal life, to universal variable life, to just variable life, to index universal life, to ten pay, twenty pay policies. There's only one of the policies that pays a dividend and that's whole life. My point, whole life insurance is the only one that pays a dividend that can be used multiple ways, such as to either increase your coverage or reduce your premium, come to you in cash. You decide each year. There are multiple uses it can have. There has been some great confusion over whether an individual should have permanent coverage or term coverage. Which one is the most beneficial? In the end, what it comes down is what coverage will be in force when you are gone. Is it important to you to have the policy in place to pay a benefit? Insurance companies sell life insurance for certain terms, like five years, ten years, or thirty years. With the name *term*, that means a certain amount of time, which doesn't necessarily mean your lifetime. Permanent whole life is for your entire life. With long-term care becoming such an issue, life insurance companies have riders to cover you. They will pay out to you a portion of the life insurance amount while you are alive, to cover certain expenses. In addition, policies can include the waiver of premium rider, which pays the premium for you if you become disabled. Insurance benefits have been enhanced, and several options are available. Therefore, it is to your benefit for you to utilize the resources of an expert in the insurance field who is knowledgeable about all of the complexities of life insurance, and then explain its benefits to you and your family.

I've studied insurance products for years and I am amazed at the product innovations that have come about over those years. However, the problem is that the latest and greatest always makes it seem as if what you already have is not enough, and that should not be the result of innovation. Generally, innovation, or the creation of a new (and sometimes better) product, creates options for its consumers. Having plenty of life insurance options should cause you to value and then weigh the options you have in order to make a determination about whether to keep the insurance you currently have or upgrade to something better.

When I realized some of the things I had purchased, that I wouldn't buy today, I got rid of them. Early in my career, and still to this day, a lot of insurance products have been constructed to compete with investments. I believe the two should be separated. Everyone should have investments, and I believe everyone should have insurance. However, you don't want to tie your insurance to an investment. It adds another level of risk that you don't need.

When you say "insurance" to most people, it is something that's guaranteed to conjure up thoughts of a type of "pie in the sky" dream of a pay out policy that has bells and whistles all over it. Generally, if people are presented with many options, they don't always take advantage of these options. When products are introduced that you are not familiar with, or you don't know if it's insurance or it's investments, or some sort of a hybrid of something else, the last thing you need is any more confusion about those options. And these bells and whistles might compromise the basic function of guaranteed insurance.

You should insure yourself properly, protect yourself against poverty, guarantee the future, and provide security both for yourself and for your family. Now, although I use the words "guarantee the future", there is truly no way anyone can guarantee anything, let alone one's future. So, what do I mean by that? Do you have enough money set aside to walk away from something that looks promising? If you do the best you can, there are certain guarantees you can have, but no one can guarantee the future. I think having faith is part of this.

Q **What are you doing today to reduce your investment risk?**

_____

_____

_____

_____

_____

_____

Q **What are you doing today to reduce your inflation risk?**

_____

_____

_____

_____

_____

_____

_____

Q **What are you doing today to reduce your life's risk?**

Q **Are you concerned more about living too long or dying too soon?**

Q **Who will be hurt financially if you can't work tomorrow?**

Chapter 5

Live Your Philosophy of Life

My philosophy all my life has been the pursuit of excellence.

— John Kluge

What is your philosophy of life? Are you a giver or taker? Oftentimes, I don't even think much about this, but when faced with an important decision we all want to make sure that we choose to do the right thing. The fact is, the decisions we make tell a great deal about who we are. What would be written about you tomorrow in the newspaper? What would be the words used to explain who you are, your life, and your philosophy?

You're philosophy of life is really about being the right kind of person, and then out of that flows the right decisions, like the use of finances. There are a variety of components to a person's philosophy of life. There's the financial side, the faith side, which is your belief system. Then there are your actions, that tell a lot about your character and whether you are teachable and capable of understanding and giving love. A combination of these things determines how we view and interpret life, and in turn, how we will choose to live it.

It all comes down to living intentionally, which I believe is the core theme of this entire book. If I should wake before I die means waking up from the typical go with the flow, not thinking one day after another, in the rut, and waking up from that to be begin living intentionally in line with your values, flowing out particularly into the realm of finances, and making sure that you're managing well what treasures you have.

Your Dollar's Value

Something I heard quite often from my grandparents growing up was "Teach your family the value of a dollar." However, nowadays this nugget of wisdom is lost to many in our society. What does that mean to value money and do we even know why is should be something to be valued? How many people throw their change at fast food or even on the ground? You may have heard this phrase before: *If you took care of the pennies, nickels, dimes, and quarters, the dollars would take care of themselves.* What does this mean? What it means is that it's the little things that can add up. Therefore, you must be cautious with the little things. Another popular money phrase is: *A bird in the hand is better than two in the bush.* I don't know where this phrase first originated from, but its message about the value of the dollar is also clear. And that message is that the value of the one thing you already have is better than two more whose value you do not know. In other words, it is better to stick with something you already have, rather than pursuing something you may never get.

Money can evoke many emotions. And emotional spending is what a lot of us end up doing. Whether it's a new outfit, new car, or anything else. So, how do we improve our lives without negatively changing our lifestyle or spending all of our money? It's called a budget. When I go on a budget, I'm going to have something less. No one does well thinking less. Everybody wants more. With working with clients, I understand that if I take something away from them, of course, I could make it better for them financially, but I can't do that because that's not going to be a long-term commitment. I have to deal with what they're currently doing and recover, find where they're losing money with what they're currently doing so that I don't impact their cash flow negatively. I don't like to use people's lifestyle money ... How do I say it? It's not a motivating reason to see someone that's going to take money out of your pocket and make your life different or worse. I don't want to change your lifestyle; I want to improve it and improve your wealth. I have to do it without impacting your lifestyle which will end up giving you more freedom, more peace of mind, more wealth, more protection, better quality of life, better relationships, peace of mind, a comfort.

You really need to understand your finances in the short-term, like what are you bringing in month-to-month, what are you spending before you can extrapolate and go long-term and figure out how much you can save. How can you use your current wealth to protect your wealth in the future? You must first have some level of understanding of what your current wealth is.

You must know how to use and pay off a credit card. This is very relevant to finances because whenever I hear the statistics about the average amount of credit card debt, I am simply blown away. Student debt is somewhere around $35,000. The total owed by average US household carrying credit card debt is $15,675. If somebody has credit card debt, they're going to have an average of $15,000 of it. The interest rates charge in most cases is above 20%. If you make the minimum payment, it'll take 30 some years to pay it off. They'll pay triple the amount that was owed. What happens is it's paid down and brought back up, paid down and brought back up, but the debt never does disappear. That's a huge wealth destroyer. People want what they want when they want it. A little payment per month isn't that painful, but it's the pennies, nickels, dimes, and quarters again. It isn't just nickels and dimes anymore; it's bigger bills and lots more money.

We're all guilty of it. It's just getting out from under it, not letting it happen again. You wouldn't have heard this either, but there used to be a time when there was no such thing as credit cards. That's where you hear your grandparents say, "We saved up for." They actually had to save the money to buy it because that was the only way you could get it. Can you imagine doing that today? Instead, the normal behavior is to buy it now because you want it and then pay it off little by little over time. Who do you think established that idea? As a result of people's impulse buying or emotionally spending money, credit card companies have become very profitable.

Financing

Most everything we buy is financed, even if we pay cash for it. However, that money could be housed somewhere else earning interest. Once people understand the concept of setting aside money to allow it to grow interest and turn into even more than its initial value, they will want to be the most efficient with their money as they can be. This is the fun part of my job, when I get to help someone do something more with their money. Together, we figure out the best strategy for them to invest their money so that it's for their benefit and not another institution's benefit.

Many, even financial experts, have said that you shouldn't use a credit card in order to stave off the risk of acquiring large amounts of debt. I disagree that you shouldn't use a credit card. Using a credit card is part of being an adult and part of being responsible to use it. The responsibility is you paying it off at the end of the month. An additional risk, alongside acquiring large amounts of debt, when using credit cards is that someone could get ahold of your card and make purchases that you have no idea about. I once used by business debit card and a month later, someone had used it in another state. They charged $800 to my card. Thankfully, the bank declined it and the fraud unit called me immediately because the card was used outside of my zip code. The benefit of a credit card is that you are financially protected if someone else uses it fraudulently. Usually the credit cards don't make you pay a fee. And if you report it lost stolen and you're not responsible for it. Part of the reason credit card companies charge so much interest though is because of fraud. They're losing millions in credit card fraud.

I wanted my kids to each have a credit card. I wanted my daughter to have her own credit card in her own name. You never know when she's going to need it. And when she got married, she and her husband had their own individual credit. I wanted the same for my son as well. The goal was for them to establish credit as soon as they could because I knew it would help when they wanted to purchase a car or purchase their first house. An established credit, whether it is good or bad, does impact certain aspects of your life. What your car insurance premium is; what interest rate you can get on your mortgage; or what you're going to pay for another loan. Your credit follows you to almost every milestone in your life.

There are a few important components that make up your credit score. The number of credit cards you have in your name and the amount of debt you have. You don't want to ever let your debt go above 30% of your allowable credit. Oftentimes, banks like for you to keep it below 10% of your allowable credit. Your payment history is also another big component. When you pay your bills in full, especially on time, this works in your favor. It's an adult responsibility to have good credit, and typically, the only way for you to establish good credit is to first have and utilize a credit card. And of course, it should be managed properly.

People usually choose credit cards based solely on the benefits that they receive from the credit card company in the form of cash back or vacations. Or maybe their favorite store will give them a discount on their purchase if they sign up. So, the scenario is that you spend $500 in products at this store and you save $50 off immediately by opening their credit card. It's real tempting to say, "Yes I want to do that." However, my advice to you is to not ever open up a credit card at a store that's offering a promotion of 10% savings on your purchase. Generally, if you do it once, you'll do it again. Before you know it, you'll end up with 20 credit cards. This will work against you in staying out of debt, and also you run the risk of losing savings when you apply for something like a car loan or a mortgage. Keep the number of credit cards you obtain limited; pay it off every month; get the rewards; and most importantly, use them wisely.

The best advice I've given to new credit card owners is what I've said before, which is to automatically apply the payment from their checking account to the credit card the day they put a charge on it. By paying ahead of the credit card bill, you won't have any surprises. Moreover, being human, there are going to be times that we will forget the amount we've already sent to pay the bill if we see something else we want to purchase. By paying off your credit card immediately, you'll know the amount of money you have in your checking account and how much you are paying out. If you can't pay for the amount you've charged on your credit card today, don't count on tomorrow's money to cover the check. The best move in a situation like this is to simply not charge the credit card.

A Snow Shield

We go through life like a snowplow does going down the road after it snows. There are obstacles in front of us that we are being bombarded with, and the blades on either side of the front of the truck are throwing the snow (and the obstacles) off to each side. However, every once in a while, the blade lifts off the ground a little and slows us down. This is what happens when we get overloaded or bombarded with a flood of financial and insurance information.

Take care of the nickels and dimes and the dollars will take care of themselves.

How do we go through life with all that stuff happening to us, with no snow shield in front of us, and still be present to be able to take it all in, let it go immediately, and make important decisions. Being able to be present and just take a deep breath to collect yourself so that you are able to make the best decision for you at the right moment is integral to improving. There's something I'm clearly aware of and it's that we are all bombarded with email, advertising, and so many other distractions. Many of us are not even always conscious of the fact that we are always being directed toward something, and it may not be in ways you'd want to be.

My definition of success is having my feet hit the ground in the morning, so I start the day with a mindset of being successful, and from there I hit the ground running. You don't want to be directed by the snow you run into, you want to direct yourself through it. That is my philosophy of life. I challenge you to think through your personal philosophy of life. A philosophy of life falls into three categories: your faith, your finances, and your family. It is important to spend time reflecting on your life—where you've come from, and your successes and failures that identify who you are. This reflection will cause you to appreciate that God has had His hands in your life from the moment you were conceived. Your family has given you both good and bad traits, traits that make up your temperament and your attitudes. Together, they create a unique combination that helps to make you a special person despite your successes and failures. Therefore, don't judge yourself by finances alone; it's just another part of what makes you unique. I encourage you to work on your strengths and have others help you with your weaknesses. The future happens if we plan for it or not. Its inevitable existence should not deter you from making effective and long-term plans for yourself and your family.

When you take control of your wealth, you won't be surprised when life happens and you have to financially plan accordingly. My goal is to see my clients take control of their wealth and add value to their lives by allowing me to lead them in the right direction toward financial investing and choosing the right insurance plan. I want to see you successful!

Chapter 6

Organize Your Financial Life

"Financial decisions made in the early stages tend to have the greatest impact on your financial wealth-creation future."

— Paul Harris

It is pretty much a guarantee in many homes that when it comes to legal paperwork or important documents we've all found ourselves buried under piles of paper. What most people do with all of their important documents, that is, is to have them all over the place, and then the importance of keeping them centrally located. Then, later in the chapter, we'll discuss all the different types of documents that you should have in this one central location. In many homes important documents and papers can be found in a junk drawer. They know what's in there, but it's not in any organized format. I've had clients who have said they have junk rooms or a junk garage where things are haphazardly placed, not readily accessible, and typically not understood completely.

Why do people need to have an actual organizational place for these important documents?

Well, the first reason for having an organized place for important personal documents is an obvious one. Essentially, if these important documents are needed quickly you need to be able to access them without hesitation. For example, medical documents could be needed immediately by a hospital or doctor to provide care. This type of document would give power to people that have the right to act on behalf of someone who is sick or dying. If they can't locate the documents, then valuable time is wasted.

Let's keep talking about why having an organized place for important documents is mandatory. I think proper management and being responsible, say a great deal about you as a planner. If you're going to go to the trouble to get the documents and put a health directive, retirement, or investment plan in place and set it up, then it should be readily accessible and easily found. Don't be sloppy about it. If important documents are needed, and you can't find them, there may be a situation where someone is waiting for an important document at a hospital and medical decisions can't get done, or people can't help you in the way you need. Therefore, it's good to have it all together in one box in case of emergency if you need to evacuate the house. Inside this box you would have trust documents, life insurance policies, deeds to real estate, certificates for stocks, also annuities, bank account numbers, safe deposit boxes, information on credit cards, unpaid taxes, and passwords for different technological accounts.

I have some clients refer to this organized place as a **hurricane box**. In case of emergencies, you've got these important documents all in one place that you can take it with you anywhere.

The Starting Line

Your box should also be organized in some sort of filing system. There are five areas that are critical to your financial success: **income, debt, protection, savings, and growth**. In the box, there should be twenty-seven places to file everything, so that those five components are broken down. Your income is labeled as your take home salary, and should include any bonuses, or residual income from rental property or secondary jobs.

The second component of your filing system is your debt. This includes debt from your mortgage to your credit cards, a car loan, student loans, home equity lines of credit, personal loans, all those are in one place broken out by what kind they are and their interest rates. Each subset of your debt has its own component as well.

When I meet with clients who want to work with me to plan their future, I always begin by requesting from them a list of items that I need. Usually, these are the obvious documents like, tax returns, wills, trusts, most recent financial statements from any accounts they have, any business agreements if they own a business, stock options, IRAs, 401ks, any annuities, any life insurance, cash statements, or money market accounts. These are all important documents that most anyone should have readily accessible. All of these documents tell my client's individual stories. The facts tell me where their story is now, and they also give details about the stories behind the story and how they got to where they are now. Every component of the organization process is done with the purpose of improving my client's stories.

If I talk to someone about their pension plan, their 401k, their IRA, or any other financial document, I then become their fiduciary. A fiduciary is a person who holds a legal or ethical relationship of trust with one or more individuals (person or group of persons). Typically, a fiduciary carefully handles money or other assets for another person. Under law, the fiduciary is required at all times to advocate for the sole benefit and interest of the one who trusts them. (Without the title of "fiduciary", I would still do anything that is in the best interest of my clients because that is the entire purpose of why I do what I do.) There are some who have been abused by professionals who claim that they were helping them with their investments and looking out for their future, but instead took advantage of them. For this reason, the Department of Labor enacted laws regarding this. As a fiduciary, I do everything in my client's best interests in order for them to create a beneficial financial future for themselves and their family.

Creating Future Options

Once, I reviewed a new client's will and the beneficiary for the wife's will was the husband, but the husband's will listed the beneficiary as himself. This isn't something that usually happens. Usually, for a husband and wife, they are indicated as each other's beneficiaries on each will. I wondered if there was some sort of mistake; a typo perhaps. Obviously there was a typo, but it was a legal document stating that he would be the beneficiary of his own assets. Needless to say it had to be fixed. Moreover, the court system would probably say that it was a typo, and the beneficiary on the husband's insurance should not have been himself but his spouse. Could it have been corrected after the fact? I don't know. Unfortunately, events beyond anyone's control occurred and the wife died, and the husband's will still named himself as the beneficiary. What if there were children who could be beneficiaries as well? Would they feel as they got swindled out of an inheritance?

If your name is in the will, you *can't* be disinherited. Things can be changed; wording or phrasing can be modified. However, if you are in the will you are not going to be disinherited. What I typically see is a husband and wife do a will and they each name each other and then the children as beneficiary. If the child is married and has children it's written as per stirpes so that if the father dies and the mother dies and leaves money to the children and one of the children is deceased but that child had children of their own, then per stirpes says that it would go to those grandchildren down the family line. One of the wills that I reviewed once wasn't this way, but quite the opposite. It left money to the three children of clients, but if one of the children had died and that child had children there would have been nothing that would have gone to them or the grandchildren. They basically would have been disinherited in the will.

By definition, per stirpes is a legal term in Latin. It reads: an estate of a decedent is distributed per stirpes if each branch of the family is to receive an equal share of an estate. Per stirpes means: My children's, children's, children. You don't disinherit unborn children or like I said if my son or daughter had children and they died why would I want to make sure it goes to them if they are not alive. It would go to their children. It's probably more than that in the legal terms but that is how I describe it. This is an example on how paramount it is to plan ahead and plan well. These things have the possibility to work against you if you don't plan.

Planning for your future should involve not only considering your will, but also inflation. The dollar that you have put away for the future has to grow at least at the rate of inflation or otherwise it'll be worth less when you use it, so part of investing is you just got to earn money on it to keep equal to inflation. Then taxes take a big bite out of your earnings depending on what your income is. I mean, obviously, the lowest is zero. First, it's 10%, and then it goes up higher than 40% in taxes. As times change, the world around us changes. New products created are affected by inflation, which affects our financial world. I'm 59, and I've seen so much change in the technology around me. I had no idea in 1986 that I'd be buying cell phones for my kids to carry around with them whenever phones came out. I mean, there was a technology cost. My parents who retired 20 years ago have iPhones. That was not a cost they planned on 20 years ago. That was a new expense and a monthly cost. It wasn't something they were considering. Whether it is technology or something else, things will happen that may be something you either need or want.

Most people can't function without new technology, so it sells and it sells quickly. Everyone is connected. We all have the internet in our homes, through our computers or iPads. In addition, technology changes so often that the technology toys we have now will be obsolete before we figure out how to use it, with the introduction of a newer and better version of the same product. Most of us don't even know what the products are going to be that we may want to purchase in the future.

Things wear out faster now than they used to. Washing machines used to last 30 years. Now we're replacing them within one-third of that time. Subsequently, people get rid of something and replace it with a new one because its life has expired faster than we'd like it to. Life happens and things change, sometimes faster than we can keep up. Nonetheless, we still have a responsibility to know what's going on around us in order to make informed decisions about our financial lives. Be conservative with the choices you make so that when things come up that you are unaware of, unfortunate things, health problems, or new technology, there are dollars available. The goal is to create options for your future and not feel trapped and constrained by financial worry. Your financial stability depends on you planning ahead.

What action(s) can you take to move closer to accomplishing your goals and living your values?

Q Are you saving enough for retirement?

Q Are you spending on areas/things that provide you little to no real value?

Chapter 7

The 15% Rule

Experiences are savings which a miser
puts aside. Wisdom is an inheritance
which a wastrel cannot exhaust.

— Karl Kraus

Everybody likes to spend money. The thing is, if you want to continue to spend money and actually have some tangible money, then you must understand how to allow that money to work on your behalf. You should live on less than you make. At a minimum, that number is fifteen percent (15%). For example, if you make $1, you've must live on $0.85. That means you're putting away, or saving, fifteen percent of your earnings. There aren't too many people whom I first meet that are anywhere near that savings amount. The goal is to get people there in our planning over time. It may not happen in a week or a month. In fact, it could take several years. The idea is that as debts get paid off start saving the money that used to be directed at your debt.

The money that you're saving, however, does have some things going against it like, inflation, taxes, and technology. That's where the 15% comes from. This is what you call financial planning. When someone tells me they're saving 15% of their income, I applaud them for their efforts. This habit is a great way to save money for your future.

Saving money for your future and the 15% rule are generally not topics that most people are familiar with. Financial education is very minimal in the country. This is an issue because most people come from not having enough already. Financial literacy can be taught, however, it's one thing to acquire this knowledge and another to apply it when your emotions are involved. Money isn't math and math isn't money. So, what makes financial education educational? When the person learning it can immediately apply that knowledge to their situation and recognize the value for themselves. There has to be something in it for them—a benefit.

People typically learn about money from their family—mostly their parents. They get this foundation sometime between when they're born until about age 14. It becomes ingrained in their brains. It is also around this time that what they have been taught determines if they will be spenders or savers. When meeting with clients, I try to understand where they learned about money and how they feel about it. Usually it's in their younger formative years where this comes about. The point is that financial literacy is necessary for you and the next generation. You should teach anyone important in your life about money and entrepreneurship.

Living on Less

The best advice I could give to a young person now is to learn to live on less than you earn. This will benefit you in the future and in the present it will help you to avoid excessive debt. Getting an education is an example of good debt, but not if the cost of the education is going to far exceed what you could earn. I say give generously. I think we as a people do give generously, but it isn't just financially, it may be more of our time than resources. Time and talent are equal.

Consider where your money is going daily and then how much you can save. It's great to have money later in life, but that "later" does not have to be in your 60s if you're smart enough to begin saving early in life.

The goal you should set is to save 15% of your income every time you get paid. This is a goal that can be difficult to start right away, however, you can at least start small. You can begin at 3% and then work your way up to the 15% number. When saving, 7.5% of that 15% should be in a 401K, IRA only. The other 7.5% should be in a place where you have easy access to the money without penalty. There are 17 other places on your financial model where money can be directed. (See the model on my website at paulharrisfinancial.com)

The amount of saving 15% can seem daunting at first, but it is based on a formula that works and will work for you. The goal—while you're saving 15% and avoiding excessive debt—is to also give generously, while you are alive, to people and to charities, and to also be hospitable.

Remember, you are thinking beyond yourself and planning a better future for the generations that will come after you.

Chapter 8

Beneficiary Benefits

Defined as one who receives a benefit of funds or other benefits, a beneficiary is the person or persons who you will want to receive the spoils (if you will) of your labor and after your death. It's important to make a list of everyone that's in your life to make sure that they're not forgotten in your planning. Why is it important to make a list? Well there are so many different investments, or ways of diversifying your finances, that the law could spell out who the beneficiary is give you the choice to name a beneficiary for everything you've put your money into. Now, keep in mind however, that the law's beneficiary may not be the same as the person you would want to be the beneficiary.

When most people think of their beneficiary they think of their life insurance beneficiary. Yet, that is not the only choice you have in beneficiaries. You can name a primary beneficiary and a contingent beneficiary for your investments. You can also name another beneficiary for your 401K, IRA or your pension. Typically when I'm working with a client and they're married I'll have the accounts be set up as "tenant by the entirety." This ensures that if either one of them passes away the other one has a hundred percent ownership of it. For the benefit of both spouses, this type of account setup garners the most profitable results.

If you have an investment account and you would like for your survivors to be the beneficiaries of those accounts upon your death then there are certain steps you need to take. One way of doing that I've seen is you become a owner with them, a joint owner with rights of survivorship, which says if mom has a checking account and daughter is on it as a joint owner then when the mother passes the account becomes one-hundred percent owned by the daughter. There are some tax ramifications, however, that need to be looked at depending on their account value and its purpose. Plus, there's another way to own accounts like these through something called Payable On Death (POD), also know as Transfer on Death (TOD). Say for example that my wife had an account in her individual name and she had a payable on death or transfer on death agreement attached to it in case of her death. The way it would work is that when she dies that account would be included in her estate and then consequently passed on to me. It would work the same way with any other account and beneficiary.

What I typically suggest to my clients is that once they've established this POD or TOD onto their account(s), this will ensure that it goes outside of probate, and directly to the beneficiary—the person who the account is payable on death or transferred on death to. Notice how I mentioned that doing this would ensure that the account goes outside of probate. This is one way you can avoid probate. I use it as a way to make everything as clean is as it can be by structuring the beneficiary properly and by pressing to my clients the importance of having a list of all the beneficiaries they can name on different accounts. A lot of clients claim their trust as beneficiary and that trust is spelled out exactly in regards to whom is going to get the money and how they're going to get it. (These trusts also detail how beneficiaries cannot get the money.)

Products that you own can also go to your beneficiary. This will depend on how the account and trust is set up. When I'm streamlining everything for my client's accounts, I like to make sure I know and they know where their money is going to go. It's a good idea to evaluate your (organized) paperwork every four years and update anything necessary. If not, it can cause a problem.

Beneficiaries are an important, if not the most important, part of planning for the future. God forbid, something happens to you too soon. Yet, it is still vital for you to have your accounts organized before anything happens. If they're not set up correctly and accurately, it can mean that your loved ones will not only lose you to death, but also lose any benefits you may had intended for them.

If someone establishes a trust and doesn't name the trust the beneficiary, the trust is then considered unfunded. Typically, without a trust, you are going to name your spouse only as the first beneficiary, then you would name a secondary, perhaps a child. (If there are no children, then you could name your parents as the second beneficiary in case something happens to your wife.)

Remember the example I talked about earlier about the wife who had left everything to her husband and the husband left everything to himself? I mentioned that obviously that was a typo and I got them to fix it after the fact. However, the lesson there was that it is imperative for you to read your own will; don't simply trust the wording or the person who prepared it, but read it for yourself. This is precisely why you need to name a specific beneficiary on your policy.

Probably one of the worst things I've seen is a participant in a 401K plan named their spouse beneficiary along with their son. However, it says plainly on the form that if it's an IRA or 401K plan your spouse must be your primary beneficiary, if not the spouse must sign off in front of a notary. Well, the husband had named his wife beneficiary of fifty-percent of the account, and his child (who was from a previous marriage) was named the beneficiary of the remaining fifty percent. However, there was no final notarized signature. After the participant passed away, his spouse claimed one-hundred percent beneficiary and since there was no signature from him saying it could be split, it all went to the wife. This meant that the child would not get the fifty-percent that the participant had intended they receive. (Well, it was either intended that way or an oversight that was not done in filing the beneficiaries.) In this situation, the person who had died assuming that their assets would be split equally, but they weren't. I actually ended up getting a call from the son, wanting to know where his benefit was. I had to break the news to him that the benefits initially intended for him to receive a portion of, would never actually go to him, and there was nothing we could do about it. The son had proof that the husband had named him his beneficiary, but it wasn't notarized and wasn't signed off by the father. Thus, the stepmother got it all. The continuation of the story is that the stepmother also had her own children from another marriage, and could list her children as the beneficiaries of her late husband's assets, and still exclude his step child. It was the worst case of not following the beneficiary rules I've seen.

This was a circumstance that I was involved in after the fact and uncovered this discrepancy in a notarized signature. When you are sitting down with me or I am going over someone's beneficiary information and I understand the family dynamics and what the client wants, you can be assured that is an area I won't tread lightly on to ensure that something like the case I just mentioned never happens again.

The law is very specific on beneficiaries and how they are to be named on the specific documents. It is critical to make sure your i's are dotted and your t's are crossed. Recently we had a client who wanted to name nieces and nephews as beneficiaries if her husband had passed, but there were a few they were concerned about when it came to how they would spend the money. We rectified this by creating an adjustment with the Trust so that there would be limitations on how much money they would get and how quickly they would get it.

Again, if trusts and beneficiaries are not done properly, everything you thought was going to happen, may very well not happen at all. If the paperwork is not done properly, with all documents carefully signed and updated, then it will be left to the courts to decide who gets your money and how it will be distributed. Believe me, you don't want the court to decide. The court has rules they have to follow in regards to dying without a will it's called intestate. Dying without a will is certainly not what most people want, even if you don't have family member(s) to name as your beneficiary, then make your beneficiary a charity. This can be done with a will or a trust.

It's important that people don't live their lives with the sole purpose of just consuming. Are we on this earth to consume or are we here to give back? If we're wrapped up in our own world sometimes we don't think about what else is going on in the world. But there is a bigger world and other causes that are going to suffer because you're not here anymore. If you know that to be true you could make a gift with your will so the organization could continue their work. What charity would you be willing to give back to? People can give back through their church or their college, or an organization they believe in.

Generally, non-profits are eager to assist their donors with ways to give money painlessly. And that's one of the things I like to work with clients on. Maybe they can't give as much as they'd like to now but they plan on giving something when their gone, and it's my job to figure out how do we structure what makes the most sense? And there's several ways to do that through a charitable remainder trust, charitable annuities, or outright gifts.

You must take an adult approach to your estate planning that leaves it in the best possible position for transfer. Don't be guilty that you left a mess for your family to deal with. This gives piece of mind knowing you've made responsible choices, taking as many steps as you can to facilitate the transfer by trust, by beneficiary, and by ownership to your family to charities you believe in.

Q **Have you taken the time to make a list of the beneficiaries on your accounts?**

Chapter 9

Personal Items

The Importance of Itemization

Just as I addressed in a previous chapter about the importance of organization, itemization follows right behind it. However, you cannot be organized unless something is itemized. When you are able to itemize your personal items, like your jewelry, for specific family members to have before you pass away, it is a gift you can leave for them that they will cherish for a very long time. You certainly don't want your passing to be wrought with bickering and arguments over who will get your gold-plaited China, or great-grandma's broach, or the antique piano. This is why it is imperative to itemize your personal and priceless items before you pass away. Planning ahead is paramount.

I had a client who would change who would receive her personal items, but she had a piano that she wanted her older son to get. The problem was that the son's second wife said she would like it. The client told me that she really wanted her older son to get it. I then pulled out a ledger and wrote down the words "piano goes to older son." Then I said, "Now tell me about the piano." From there it went a little further than the piano to a necklace and a lamp that she wanted specifically to go to three different people in her family.

During the rest of that meeting, she went on to describe every detail of that piano—its dimensions, color, and any imperfections. She did the same thing with the necklace and the same thing with the lamp. You may also have mementos that maybe don't have any value monetarily, but they have a value in memory.

When you create this itemized list make sure it spells out exactly who gets what. And usually that is housed with the client's important papers. One thing I've debated on is when family members, two or more of the children want something and it's not been decided who gets it. If they can't decide then it will be sold at an auction and they will split the money. Obviously there's a motivation for them to agree, but it must be their decision. Another thing I've had people do is give the items beforehand just so there's no question in whose possession it is. Sometimes, I could have these items years before. There may be particular items that you may want to keep in the family. Itemization helps to keep your exact wishes for who will have what.

The True Meaning of Giving a Gift

A gift is giving something of yourself, an item that comes from you that you have thoughtfully considered to give to someone else to remember you by. This is a gift that only you can give. It is something of great value to you that will eventually become of great value to the person who receives it. It could be equal, it could be a little less, or it could be even more valuable to them. What a wonderful feeling it is to be able to give someone a valuable gift such as this while you are alive. And also to see how the person treats it.

So what are the gifts only you can give? The love part, this is having the opportunity to give someone a gift that shows them that you love them. And having them enjoy it while you are still alive. In my own life I have done that. I've done it by raising kids, as any parent would say. And actually, it's the most joyous thing I could do. I have great memories of being able to do things for my kids.

You may have items like that gold watch you may have in your jewelry box, that you've wondered who you should leave that to. Well, you have the option of selling and getting the cash now. Or you could put that special watch on the list and decide whom you would give it to. I personally have twenty-seven items on my list, and I have six brothers and sisters, two kids, and a wife. Then, there's mom and dad, nieces and nephews, and others in the family. And I think you know, it would be prudent to say that there may be other people other than your immediate family that you would want things to go to.

You may even decide to give these valuable items to your loved ones while you are still here with them. People don't want to deal with it, but the truth is that we are all eventually going to die one day. However, the best thing you can do is live your life to the fullest right now, so why not give your loved ones these valuable personal items while you're alive. The majority of people don't do this type of planning because they don't want to think about it. But the cost of doing it is high compared to what the cost would be without doing it, both financially as well as emotionally for those who are left behind.

Gift giving is an action that causes us to take a moment or two of reflection on our lives and on those that we love. I'm better for myself, and also in my faith and with my clients when I'm able to see gift giving as an opportunity to love others and connect with those who are close to me. And what a great opportunity I have to discuss and address this topic of gift giving with my clients as well.

Over my career, I've seen clients die, I've had people get disabled, I've had people lose jobs, I've seen divorces, etc. I've seen almost every imaginable kind of thing happen to people that they didn't expect. Through all of these experiences and many other different factors, I've learned that there's nothing more valuable than going through an experience instead of just reading about it or studying it. You must actually work through the problems because obviously there's raw emotion: what was said, what needed to be done, what was set up, how do we handle this, what are the decisions or ramifications and how they will be treated when the person needs healthcare? This is where the rubber meets the road, if you will.

I know I've had a dramatic impact on people's lives because of what I do. I know how to advise on retirement and life decisions. The clients I work with only get these experiences once, and I believe that I'm there with them to ensure that they don't squander their one shot. Through the vast number of clients that I've worked with, seeing the before and the after repeatedly, I know that I can help people to do it right the first time.

Wooden Box

Years ago I had a potential client come in, and I made my presentation of the services I provide. When speaking to clients about my services, I also give them useful advice on the best ways to organize important documents and personal items by putting them into a wooden box.

The box I use has 27 components: 9 protection; 9 savings; 9 growth. All of these components are how I organize your important documents. They will include passwords for email addresses, important websites, and bank accounts. Also, insurance documents, notarized trusts, wills, and more. I prepare this box for each of my clients and give it to them after I've organized their documents. It makes it easy to keep your documents organized!

Personal Items I bequeath to:

Date: _____

Signature: _____

Chapter 10

Make Your Legacy Count

"It is up to us to live up to the legacy that was left for us, and to leave a legacy that is worthy of our children and of future generations."

— Christine Gregoire

Letters Never Written, Words Not Spoken

The creation of this last chapter was for a specific purpose, in that I wanted it to cause you to contemplate your life and your loved ones. Words are powerful and have the ability to permanently change someone's life. What are the words that you have not yet spoken or the letters never written to your loved ones that you *need* to say to them? Hmm, it is something to seriously think about, isn't it?

Have you ever thought of some heartfelt words that you may have wanted to say to someone you loved, but missed your opportunity? Perhaps it may have not been the right moment to say anything or you lost their address and could not write them a letter, or it may have been that you simply didn't have the right words to say or put on paper. These letters will represent a reflection of your life and you have to think about what you need to do. They will be less about finances and insurance planning and more about you.

The Bible has been published more than any other book ever in history. Are there things in our personal life that should be published as well for one generation to carry on to the next? It is important to write down the things you've learned and convey those lessons to the next generation who are watching you. History repeats itself, but it all depends on what is being repeated. So what do you learn the first time that will be valuable to teach someone else? We seem to believe, well this time it's different. And in some ways there are little differences, but there are some things that continue to happen.

Your happiest moments are a time of reflecting on your life and your experiences. We have all had plenty of experiences throughout our lives that we can share with others as lessons for life. Take the time to write those down for future generations to know. The objective is that you are being present and able to tell your family what they mean to you. Those moments where you say things like: "I miss you when I leave," "I love you when you get home," "You are valuable to me." Is there anyone that you would like to share your heart with and let them know how much they mean to you before you pass away? Don't delay; do it now. It will be time well spent.

Create Your Legacy Fund

Before we talk about creating a legacy fund, let's first dissect the intricate parts of a legacy fund. A legacy is an inheritance you leave behind for your children's children. No matter what form the legacy is in, whether it is a family business, money, or an estate, it is something that you are giving back to the next generation. A legacy is an extension of yourself. So, the idea of a legacy fund is that when you are no longer here, you have something to extend to your loved ones. What have you set up to create some type of legacy to tie the family together? It could be within part of the beliefs and knowledge you taught them. Maybe you set up a fund that is only to be used for charity and your family is on the board making decisions on where this money should go. That teaches them business sense and what their dollars are doing.

If there is something that can be transferred from one generation to the next, that doesn't have anything to do with technology, cars, anything, that are just fundamental beliefs and truths that they learned during their life. They can pass on to the future. Think about what those things are. Do not be only a consumer, but also a participator in life.

Will you choose to only be a consumer in this world, or will you choose to be a giver? The decision is in your hands, and it requires your action.

Final Words

Why I Wrote This Book

Believe it or not, there is a particular reason why I made the decision to write this book. I did it to help people like you organize and optimize their financial, legal, and personal history all in one place to establish a benchmark to follow to unlock all of the steps necessary to have a life of purpose and without regret. Wow, that was a mouthful! And it is all true. I want you to improve your world and the worlds of your loved ones.

I've had the privilege to work with many clients who have pushed through the process to improve their legacy. The world is full of information that can become deafening and overload our minds and our choices. The analogy I use to explain the onslaught of information is to imagine a snowplow driving down the street with the plow just a fraction of an inch above the ground. This snowplow is pushing aside all the information. If the driver raises the plow, then information will get in. However, without some way to process the information the snowplow will stop. We need information, and we have to have it. Yet, too much information will cause us to stop and feel overwhelmed. Moreover, we don't take in enough information and it will cause us to miss the meaning or truth. What this snowplow model indicates is that everything has its place and its purpose is self-evident.

Once the information is learned, the why, how, what, when, and where come alive and assist you in making your best decisions. Your time is the most important element needed. In fact, your thoughts, concerns ambitions, sacrifices, opportunities, ambitions, strengths families, health, outlook, and future are all on the line. Don't leave it up to the government or financial institutions to direct your life.

Make the decision to take control of your wealth

I'd like to thank you for letting me share a little about myself with you and about my experiences in financial planning and legacy planning. My hope is that you have not only learned a few things from the chapters of this book, but that you have also been encouraged and challenged to action to create a legacy for generations after you.

Now I challenge you to act!

What will you do next?

Contact me at paul@paulharrisfinancial.com or 239-939-5131 and say you want to get started! I'll be there for you. Or you can write to me at 4560 Via Royale, Suite 4B Fort Myers, FL 33919-1076. Or you can follow me on Facebook, Twitter or LinkedIn.

About the Author

In 1981, Paul A. Harris started what has grown to "Paul Harris Financial." His clients are successful individuals, families, professionals and business owners.

Paul has built his company to help clients to be clear and excited about their personal future, thus enabling them to make strategic decisions with their finances that are crucial to their future well-being and peace of mind.

After graduating from Florida State University in 1980 with a business degree in marketing, he worked as a Pension Administrator, Life Insurance Sales and Business Owner. In 1986 he received the Chartered Life Underwriter (CLU) designation and later earned the Chartered Financial Consultant designation (ChFC). Most recently Paul has also added the Chartered Advisor for Senior Living (CASL) designation to his impressive list of accomplishments. He has his Life, Health, Variable Annuity Licenses and Security Licenses 6, 22, 63 & 65.

Paul married Suzanne in 1983. They have two children, Ryan and Ashley.